AS

YET

AS

YET

Todd Baron

chax press 2012

ISBN 9780925904 19 5

Library of Congress Catalouging-in-Publication Data

The Author would like to thank the editors and pubishers of the *The Something-or-Other*, *The Whatchamacallit* (Whozi-whatsit Press), and last but not least my his mom, for work on some of these poems.

Chax Press
411 N. Seventh Avenue
Tucson Arizona 85705-8388
USA

to Sophie Dylan Baron

contents

Poem (for marianne moore)

So, he who strongly feels
Behaves

Stands from
upon himself
Who

himself
Reverts not

Form, but

To find as rather
Not to say

Domestic

                From here
The language sounds like anything.
(Falls to the floor, screams
The name aloud
Like sudden rain or
dogs across
The street. Next door,
Trimmed by someone other
Than the gate,
The hammer's
Finishing
Instead of playing

*

If one cell finished the next
If one cell sd something
Regarding sound. If one remarked
The trees
Are in season, too.
AS IF I'm home
in the word "however"

*

The computer says
It looked
Like fun. the fairy sd
I live in this forest
What's yr excuse?

Mine *(for RD)*

The planting of clover
& burning root & home

precisely AS IF
only a few notes

we think
of as process

document & stable
leaving instigating

revival

against (What
ever it is) which

runs perception AS
IF (at all) that mattered

Or Of what
Could be

Germination—

what could be the
Sound germinating

One would have to have

A horn for that,
Or advent of
Intent, image of

Intent, precisely
Making sound

Out In Reality

There is no "telling

Each by each" except literal

Transportation .

"Everyday I see

A little more of how hard this is..."

Invisible Comix .1

It's a great war
Akin them   the dog's howling
Inside
Me or you suspended
Reversal
Towards
Movement in space or structure

Compression that
Aimlessly sounds
The ground
Slow enough
In place

Dog's heart
The image of
(color) (sound)

Invisible Comix.2

    And the surface overreaching
Image of the page

Now a "motion" picture
Senor not replicant

drawing into b/w
like a leak, the work

"like they really act
like that" reminding

disorder

Stitch *(for Sophie)*

Water—?

Concrete moves

Faster, slides

Even

Cracks. It's the

Thing itself that

"enters into it

Only as an image." No,

That isn't it

I call it

What is real

Annihilate them

With weapons (if

It is a sea) looking out

From under itself. Cantilever of

Symbols merely

space

Approximate reinforcement

Fluid, later

Indifference or doubt the scenario

Passing future

planting

& reading what comes next

+ Therapy

I have been accused
Of being Direct, likeable
Posturing in an age of
Guttural negations
Cutting through what's left
Of the table next to wine
And the keys left
Therein; aftermath
Of sudden downpour, cramps
Put me to sleep-the rest
Is rest

*

Were you looking for
An emegerency, or
Did you find one?
That's the cause for
Anything but doubt, the DVD
In your hand speaks
Of vibrations, woods in
The woods, *vibrations.*
Is that what you want
To be remembered for
Musically, anyway?
Appealing to your
Common sense?

*

You've got me
Writing this down, now
Last night you'd left
Me in a pool of dreams—corny
But reality sank
Like an amber
Pistol, what-
ever

*

Each letter expresses
Spontaneous combustion, maybe
Just maybe, the last dinner
you remember didn't
agree with me, but what the
hell—you
never stop talking, I
on the hand, hide
till it goes away

*

All pretty normal, let's
Wait to see what happens,
Maybe nothing at all
Or a permanent basin
will fill the sand
next to your
feet.

Partition(s)

The obvious, overstated

—Marriage,
pragmatic

As if they were new
" I'll live in the sky
"When work is
Done,
Down- in -the -valley"

A poem for you if you wrote it

(For Sophie)

Can't build it, finger
job, giant
Bug
          House
River bank scene
To paint
Query or questioning
Screen with teeth
Needing just to
Do this for a minute, too.
But spud, hey
You're remembering
The past, a dreary
comic tying
knot saves me
From the model
Sigh. It's
All uphill
Eating special effects or
Royalty on
knees, perhaps
I can help you now, how
Do You Spell That
And how you
Draw what
Comes next

(vintage strip)

And face to face
w/out
Intent

(is it?) curiously
shadow'd

parallel
amplitude
day

Adultery 2

From here

The language sounds like anything.

(Falls

To the floor, screams

Like sudden rain, er

Smog across

The street, Trimmed by some other

Gate, instead of playing,

It's domestically

Brings so many

Years to others.

Invisible Comix. 6

Without being seen

She called me

- The Next day I

Was not very big

& I wondered

How I got it

Box'd (copy)

Selections is arbitrary,
Unlike nature. "*America*"

killing its youth. Aftermath of
Year of teaching

Uncertainty or doubt. "look under
Murder"
Enclosed in
thermals.

I heard it on the radio now

            Light against
Cheap blue
Mist, O

Dawn's
Holding two swords
Once was
shelter

I'm outta here: Repetition

1.

Humiliation?

The temperate hand

History repeats
Not only itself
The mathematician
(white and black

borders in a time of

(police citation) seeks last
night's trust / I

was dreaming

    ex-postulate

if over, then, the
station's seeking new
forms today

    parking
lot's air conditioned/jazz
rendition of
"teen spirit" the
news

in order to
pay adheres to
a code
describing a number

"supernatural plot"
beginning with
"a"
not in
sequential order

you think it's all trash
this/beginning
with "you"

2.

As if there were any doubt
I, too, grew up in a Valley

        The bank
Subsidized my
Allocation

        The problem was
There were no Ants
Who would go to war

        They photographed
our information
as if they were people

((you)) in a series
of metaphoric vibrations

the sun's repetition
comes to the shore

"let's deep fry them"

Call this occasion to order

        each extension
the next flag
unparticular exploitation
of form

the temblor hits

these photographs are ourselves

not wanting to emulate our
common link
to traitors

3.

It's not you I'm calling

It's as if
We met

Others can only debate
the fastest growing
Pattern of regret

                    "supernatural pattern of
plot evolved from
repetitious treatment of
others

          yes, in a series of dynamic
team players, the transitional
cease to exist

I could name you by name any
one of you 300 underrepresented
vertebrate species

But so far I find myself
          admitting
To Transmission

Become hostages

We cease to admit

Division. a

Memory in forms of forestalling

Images in which suction
ACTS AS

Non descript
Cauterization, it's all

In a shadow second positioning
Posit pig latin as real
Decay

The shirt goes to waste
If not the war

The throat continues to
reflect
As if

Even one human thing
Were not numbered

In creation of
Actual doubt

Don't touch the page

Somewhere between
loading the song

Décor of light

Mere custodial
wet ground

Between water

Dynamism (motif)

Catching rhythms of

"What doesn't smell" if

All the inhabitants

were doors.

Text messaging is

Composition

It's this moment

of reading imagery

AS If (I'd) (therefore) (go) (into) The Body

Lying in sun

The pages

turn (upon) itself (as) (if) (there I go again)

contually

standing in

water.

AS IF to say (there) (I) (go again) no matter, really.

simply *far*

between motifs

        And plain

Authenticity

Of doubt

Hermeneutic

            Say something

Robotic, America. Make the

Little man

Go away. It's

an act of

Fruition tied to

Singular Rime

in the middle

Of gardening.

            The bloom

The hand, parenthetically

Clinging to the meta-

phonic appearance.

What happens

Establishes the right

Of gesture . What

Would be

The right to

Ourselves,

Anyway.

Tributary (Comix .4)

G was attempting
To look like me

An ocean out of razor blades

Out of the Atom
A sequence of pairs

Illustrating my

Rom

As if material
Lifted me, er

The cat

The Political movement, the
Middle class   this

Humiliation (he sd)
Stronger then interstitials

Not the stem
Or flower

Ironic Ex cohabiters
A handful

Of dice
Bathing in mother's sink

All that's left is gold
Modulated by Imitation

I would have betrayed
The other music

Because he
Sd it was dry

A super natural plot

Wrestling with
(Indifferent) sections

I had nothing
To do

With it but
Rocked right along
With it

If you want to say something
About your past

Drive it
To the desert

It's not as if
I needed a brain

To clean up this mess

That's the reasons it
Actually gets in

You're like
Completely inconsequential

Like the thing itself
Under the shade, what

To do what to

Do the thing
Appearances settle

comix. 5

It's Reversible
which
Refutes the juice

"just

Talking"

That slip of dice
About "you"

Which is true
(the
effect)
(which

We stick to

What
Ever

Every so often
It's the
Same thing

Lands on you

twice

*lo fi

It, being Impatient
Tranquil, ordained
Jubilant
meaning towards
invention, (another
World for
Word for
Word that is (silent
drawing up close
objects, which are cool,
Muscles
response.

Elegies

#1 *(satire)*

any mind doesn't know
what it talks about

broken by rhythm in the middle
of a beat—
comes into the room

no matter how short it is(as

really everything that anyone says
inside their heads—

what sounds like a bridge
or interlude (and

what's meant to be said
by even the smallest figure

#2 *(Jimmy Scott)*

worried
that the question
proceeds an answer

the rhythm of the swing—always

so that when he does

he dies,
a little, too

#3 *(protean)*

there was always some thing
needing to be said or ingested

the ring of the mouth to shift, wandering

a little hum
between somatic distress

#4 *(Benny Goodman)*

division of threat
(fear?) (labor?)

a line of timber
placed between a ship, revision

of self, spatial
equivalents — that shape

cumulative — preface unraveling
common ground — the mouth

river or bridge, disposition
as subject-sound

out of the wind
the branches

make it
live

the odd wood, then
older river

#5 *(song)*

the sister inside his body—
repeatedly—hung as a head should be—

which is where they go
or where they want to go

after they get there.
the one that doesn't spill memory.

"there's a lump on the bed
or in it" *the point is to make*
others see

#6 *(chet)*

what we wear is what the difference is—

Hey, what's happening.

if it were a sunny day the wind
masks some particular—. what's

pretending to be
—hurts

the identification
of the equivalent

we vowed to grasp

#7 *(Ah, Bird)*

pharmacology is atmospheric
detention, one

day shifts to the next.

shifts on top of the next

morning, &
life,

almost like every other picture.

naturally, it's

geology —

between you and
the sun.

#8 *(Glenn Gould)*

g-d's the
dimmest bulb
in the sky,
but only because
the idea
is remembered—

#9 *(boy bands)*

correspondingly small roots and
the speed at which they penetrate

like dam'd odd epiphytitic ferns
where we have only been like cold odd ferns

like the curtain in a web of curtains
of ice

like being held or trying to get
into a movie

where giants spiders are epiphanies, where
whether or not this is

good for us the door's wide open
like this house is made of water & over here

the air's commodified
like there's even a chance there'll be

this kinda stuff, like an apostrophe
covered in news of approaching glass

there lines might carry

#10 *(Joan Baez)*

slap in the face
equals lyric exposition

TV on & across
the surface of the page

or, as someone once sd
we have a right to grumble

in the here and now

#11 *(Rachmaninoff Not Frank O'Hara)*

nobody owns
anything of quality

foreground for forbearance

or thought

won't get past the

personal
concert
            to push
                backwards
towards the Prussian

"well, we are"
born to some degree

            a virtual bed
when our
drinks run out

#12 *(song for hunter s thompson)*

it is always that
novel flow

or narrative human
drift

which ceases to astound
from its professional cliff

*

Screens

Initials air

Canonization   speech

Tempered

climate

Beneath sun

Another

Degradation

Changes

school

Loss of

large white

Temperament

Roots, even

He would say

Dangling

- GRACE OF

LIVING CLEAN

Speaks quietly

“where they

‘have been”

water -

negative electric

Wisp *(invisible comix for Robin Blaser)*

The planting, & burnt wood
& fiber. The curve of hand

Around the ditch, the rain
Around the hand — dark

In the hand that
Does the planting

Of the fiber
By the ditch.

Or given by name (AS
Planting by seed, random-

ly by doubles, random
As they return

To where they
Progressed, To where

They ditch
The ditch

In circles
Of water.

As if light sources

were
IT

& “wonderful sorrow”.

(the thought of ideas in invisible comics)

Just to let you know

We were once

In it, too, that we

Could catch

The rhythm in

Dull as day

*

Or that we heard
The view

And liked it,

Anyway.

*

about the author

Todd Baron is the author of *Outside* (Avenue B Books), *Tell* (Texture Press), *This...Seasonal Journal* (paradigm press), Return of the World (O Books), *Partials* (e.g. press), *Dark as a Hat* (abacus, Poets and Poets), *That Looks At One and Speaks* (Factory School), and *TV eye* (Chax Press). In 1982 he co-founded (along with Tosh Berman) *ISSUE* magazine. in 1990 he co-founded (with Carolyn Kemp) *ReMap* Magazine. His work as appeared in various journals including *Hambone, Sulfur, Apex of the M, Temblor, Acts, New American Writing, Mandorla, the Washington Review, RiBot* and *The Gertrude Stein Awards for Innovative Writing* (1991). He was also one of the founding members of Littoral Books.

Chax Press

Chax Press is a 501(c)(3) nonprofit organization, founded in 1984, that has published more than 130 books, including fine art editions and trade editions of literature and book arts works.

For more information, please see our web site at *http://chax.org*

Chax Press is supported by individul contributions, and in part by the Tucson Pima Art Council and the Arizona Commision on the Arts, with funds from the State of Arizona and the National Endowment for the Arts.